Praying with the Jesuits

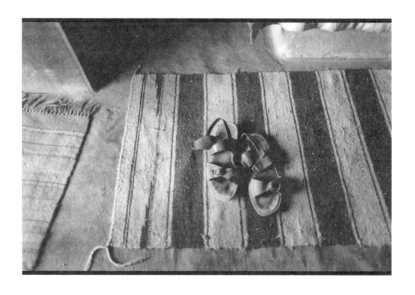

Praying with the Jesuits

Finding God in All Things

Charles J. Healey, SJ

Foreword by James Martin, SJ

Paulist Press
New York/ Mahwah, NJ

Cover and book design by Lynn Else

IMPRIMI POTEST
Rev. Myles N. Sheehan, SJ
Provincial, New England Province of the Society of Jesus
November 6, 2009

Cover and interior photographs by Rev. Michael Flecky, SJ; used with permission
of the photographer. The sculpture on the cover, "Ignatius of Loyola (1491–1556):
Founder of the Society of Jesus: Soldier, Scholar, Saint," is by Littleton Alston.

The prayers of Karl Rahner on pages 41–42, 60, 63, 65, and 75 are taken from Karl
Rahner, *Prayers for a Lifetime* (New York: Crossroad Publishing, 1984). Used with
permission of the publisher.

"I Love Your Promise/Psalm 119" by Daniel Berrigan is from Daniel Berrigan,
Uncommon Prayer, A Book of Psalms (Maryknoll, NY: Orbis Books, 1998). Used
with permission of the author.

Excerpts from *Walking Humbly: Scripture Meditations in Verse*, by Thomas Flowers.
Copyright © 2009 by Thomas Flowers, Paulist Press, Mahwah, NJ. Reprinted by
permission of Paulist Press, www.paulistpress.com.

Library of Congress Cataloging-in-Publication Data
Healey, Charles J.
    Praying with the Jesuits : finding God in all things / Charles J. Healey; foreword
by James Martin.
      p. cm.
    ISBN 978-0-8091-4697-0 (alk. paper)
    1. Jesuits—Spiritual life. 2. Jesuits. 3. Ignatius, of Loyola, Saint, 1491–1556.
Exercitia spiritualia. 4. Ignatius, of Loyola, Saint, 1491–1556. 5. Spiritual life—
Catholic Church. 6. Prayer—Catholic Church. I. Title.
    BX3703.H43 2011
    248.4′82—dc22

                                                                         2010044160

Published by Paulist Press
997 Macarthur Boulevard
Mahwah, New Jersey 07430

www.paulistpress.com

Printed and bound in the
United States of America

DEDICATION

In loving memory of

Richard T. Cleary, SJ

(1932–2009)

and

Thomas P. O'Malley, SJ

(1930–2009)

O sing to the LORD a new song;
   sing to the LORD, all the earth!
Sing to the LORD, bless his name;
   tell of his salvation from day to day.
                              (Psalm 96:1–2)

Contents

Foreword

Most people who seek to understand what has come to be called "Ignatian spirituality"—that is, the spirituality flowing from the life and the writings of St. Ignatius Loyola—turn to three main sources.

The first is his great spiritual classic, the *Spiritual Exercises*, a sort of manual for a four-week retreat based on the life of Jesus Christ. The second is the Jesuit *Constitutions*, which sets out the rules and regulations governing the life of men in the Society of Jesus, founded in 1540, as well as the other founding documents of the Jesuit order. Third is the saint's personal journals and letters, which offer us a unique window into his own spiritual life and the way he helped others in theirs.

But as the Jesuit historian John W. O'Malley notes in his superb book *The First Jesuits*, there is at least one other way of understanding the foundations of Ignatian spirituality, and that is the activities of the early Jesuit priests and brothers. So, for example, knowing that Ignatius and the "early companions" opened up a home for reformed prostitutes and founded schools for young men tells us just as much about their ideal of "finding God in all things," as any document can.

Charles J. Healey's new book, *Praying with the Jesuits*, reminds us of a further way of understanding Ignatian spirituality: the inner lives of the men who followed Ignatius, and also the special devotions of Jesuits throughout history.

So, in addition to selections from the *Spiritual Exercises*, we are introduced to the spirituality of such Jesuit heroes as

St. Francis Xavier and Blessed Peter Faber, both close friends of Ignatius. But the book focuses not just on his early companions but also on later Jesuits like St. Edmund Campion, St. Claude la Colombière, and Gerard Manley Hopkins. Also included are the prayers and insights of those you might call "modern Jesuits," such as Pedro Arrupe, Pierre Teilhard de Chardin, Henri de Lubac, Daniel Lord, and Avery Dulles. Some of these towering figures you may know; others you may not. All are worth hearing from.

Reading this book is a marvelous way to meet Ignatius, his close friends, and some of the great Jesuits that have brightened the history of the Society of Jesus. But it is also a way for you to meet God in a new way, because *our* relationship to God is always deepened whenever we listen to others talk about *their* relationship with God. It's a bit like a relationship with a close friend. No matter how well you know him or her, listening to another friend talk about how much your friend is loved always highlights aspects of your friend that you might have overlooked.

So, for example, when we read Pierre Teilhard de Chardin speaking of God as the "Saviour of human unity," we learn something new about God. When we hear Bernard Lonergan talk of God's love as the "crowning point of our self-transcendence," we learn something more. And when we read Karl Rahner's belief that "only in love" can we find God, we learn even more.

What's the best way to read this gem of a book? Slowly. Each selection could provide enough content for meditation and prayer for a whole day. So don't rush.

To use a favorite word of Ignatius, let yourself "savor" these passages, and allow yourself to find God here and in all things.

James Martin, SJ
July 2010

Introduction

Any treatment of Jesuit prayer or spirituality must begin with the founder of the Society of Jesus (Jesuits), St. Ignatius of Loyola (c. 1491-1556). His early military career and worldly aspirations as a Spanish courtier came to an abrupt end when a cannonball seriously injured his legs in a battle between Spanish and French soldiers at Pamplona in Spain in 1521. The extended period of convalescence that followed was a critical time for the young soldier, since it led to a profound experience of God and his subsequent conversion. Ignatius emerged from his sickbed at Loyola castle in Spain a profoundly changed person. Moved by God's abundant grace during that period of recovery, he would go on to commit himself generously to God's service with that energy and devotion with which he had previously pursued his courtly and military career.

A number of years would pass, however, before God's will became clear for Ignatius. Years of pilgrimage and spiritual growth would take him to many different places until he settled in Rome to serve his newly founded order as superior general. In the early stages of this spiritual journey, he first visited the Benedictine monastery of Montserrat in Spain for some days of prayer and retreat and then continued to the nearby town of Manresa, where he devoted almost a year to prayer and penitential practices. These times of abundant graces and growth prepared him well for a devout but hazardous journey and pilgrimage to the Holy Land.

The pilgrimage to Jerusalem left Ignatius with the realization that he would need further education if he were to be effective in God's service. This led to early studies at Barcelona, Alcala, and Salamanca in Spain and then on to

3

years of study at the famed University of Paris. At Paris he inspired Blessed Peter Faber, St. Francis Xavier, and a small band of other students to join him, and together they decided that after their studies they would remain together as a group and go and work in the Holy Land for the conversion of the Muslims. On August 15, 1534, the feast of the Assumption of the Virgin Mary, the small but united band of graduate students confirmed these holy desires at the Mass they celebrated together at the small chapel dedicated to Saint Denis on the slope of Montmartre. The decision to form a religious order with St. Ignatius at its head still lay in the future, but the vows pronounced at Montmartre were an important step.

By early 1539, however, it became clear that the ten "pilgrim priests" would not be able to go to the Holy Land, and so they decided to gather at Rome, offer their services to the pope, and express their willingness to go to the Indies or any other part of the world where there was an apostolic need. The group also decided, after much prayer and deliberation, to form a new religious order. Ignatius drew up the document that summarized the purpose and aim of the group; it contained in seed form the main points that would be developed more fully in the later *Constitutions* of the Society of Jesus, namely, the strong apostolic dimension, loyalty to the Holy See, a readiness to go anywhere in the world, a prompt and persevering obedience to the superior that they would elect from the group, and the foregoing of the traditional chanting of the Divine Office for the interest of the apostolate. It was a new and pioneering type of religious order and one well suited to the needs of the church at the time, with its stress on mobility and flexibility. The document received papal approval in 1540 and shortly afterward Ignatius was elected the first superior general.

Ignatius remained in Rome until his death in 1556 as the religious leader and superior of the Jesuits, who now were traveling to all parts of Europe and the world beyond to spread the good news of Christ. During these years their number grew from ten to a thousand and it would continue to grow. The needs were great, for this was one of those times in history that was marked by major change and turmoil. The new order's stress on apostolic endeavors and loving and generous service in the spread of Christ's kingdom on earth made it aptly suitable to meet the challenges of the times. In addition to his role as religious leader, Ignatius labored to write the *Constitutions* of the Society that were needed to delineate the "way of proceeding" that would characterize the aim and purpose of its members. He also put the final touches to the *Spiritual Exercises* that would always be the primary source of Jesuit prayer and spirituality.

Praying with the Jesuits seeks to share the heritage of Jesuit prayer that has emerged over the past five hundred seventy years. It is expressed in the sources of Jesuit prayer, especially the *Spiritual Exercises*, and in the prayers and reflections of individual Jesuits. It can also be found in the devotions that have been associated with Jesuit spirituality and the Society's particular way of proceeding that is rooted in the *Constitutions* of the Society of Jesus and the documents of its general congregations.

The prayer long associated with St. Ignatius sums up the spirit that should motivate the Jesuit in his prayer and apostolic service.

> Lord Jesus, teach me to be generous;
> teach me to serve you as you deserve,
> to give and not to count the cost,
> to fight and not to heed the wounds,
> to toil and not to seek for rest,
> to labor and not ask for reward,
> except that of knowing that I am doing your will.
>
> Amen.

The Spiritual Exercises

The Spiritual Exercises *occupy a central place in Jesuit prayer and spirituality. Their origins go back to St. Ignatius's own prayerful experiences and to his growing awareness after his conversion of the many ways God's grace was working powerfully in his life. The notes he kept of these graces and insights during his days at Manresa form the basis of this spiritual classic that Ignatius continued to revise and amplify until the work's definitive publication in 1548. During his years of study in Spain and at Paris, he used the* Spiritual Exercises *to assist many who were seeking a deeper relationship with God in ways that were adapted to their needs. The* Spiritual Exercises *were given in their full form to such early companions as Francis Xavier and Peter Faber and the others in the group who formed the founding fathers of the new order. Among the apostolic works that occupied the early Jesuits, the giving of the* Spiritual Exercises *immediately became one of the primary ministries.*

The purpose of the Spiritual Exercises *is to bring about a very active and generous conformity to the will of God. They are simply a series of spiritual exercises—meditations, considerations, and contemplations—that the individual makes in a context of prayer under the guidance of a director. They seek to free persons from inordinate attachments and disorders so that they might be free to surrender to the call of grace in seeking, finding, and accomplishing God's will in their lives.*

The main text of the Spiritual Exercises *is divided into what Ignatius referred to as four weeks. The first week seeks to bring a person to a deeper understanding of being a forgiven sinner through experiencing God's mercy and compas-*

sion. The second focuses on the following of Christ and aims to bring a person to a generous and full response to God's personal call. The exercises of the third week are given to a contemplation of Christ's passion and death, and the fourth week centers on Christ's resurrection. Overlapping these weeks are two very significant exercises: the Principle and Foundation at the beginning of the first week and the Contemplation to Attain Divine Love at the end of the fourth week.

St. Ignatius had no intention of writing a systematic study of prayer in the Spiritual Exercises, but he does suggest a number of different ways of approaching God in prayer. He wanted primarily to assist others while they were making the Spiritual Exercises but he also realized that the benefits gained during the days of retreat could easily be extended to one's prayer in the future. Thus, we can speak of the Spiritual Exercises as a "school of prayer."

It should also be emphasized that Ignatian prayer is marked by an outward thrust. Ignatius wanted prayer to be integrated with one's work and daily activities, and he was constantly encouraging others to meet the challenge of harmonizing their work and their prayer. This goal of integration is summed up in the familiar Ignatian phrases "finding God in all things" and being a "contemplative in action."

Soul of Christ (Anima Christi)

Soul of Christ, sanctify me.
Body of Christ, save me.
Blood of Christ, inebriate me.
Water from the side of Christ, wash me.
Passion of Christ, strengthen me.
O good Jesus, hear me.
Within your wounds hide me.
Permit me not to be separated from you.
From the wicked foe defend me.

At the hour of my death call me.
And bid me come to You.
That with Your saints I may praise You
Forever and ever. Amen.

(This was a favorite prayer of St. Ignatius and is often placed at the beginning of the text of the Spiritual Exercises.*)*

Spiritual Exercises

By the term Spiritual Exercises we mean every method of examination of conscience, meditation, contemplation, vocal or mental, and other spiritual activities, such as will be mentioned later. For, just as taking a walk, traveling on foot, and running are physical exercises, so is the name of spiritual exercises given to any means of preparing and disposing our soul to rid itself of all its disordered affections and then, after their removal, of seeking and finding God's will in the ordering of our life for the salvation of our soul.

—Sp. Ex., # 1

Savoring Deeply

For, what fills and satisfies the soul consists, not in knowing much, but in our understanding the realities profoundly and savoring them interiorly.

—Sp. Ex., #2

A Generous Heart

The persons who receive the Exercises will benefit greatly by entering upon them with great spirit and generosity toward their Creator and Lord, and by offering all their desires and freedom to him so that His Divine Majesty can make use of their persons and of all they possess in whatsoever way is in accord with his most holy will.

—Sp. Ex., #5

God's Action

During these Spiritual Exercises when a person is seeking God's will, it is more appropriate and far better that the Creator and Lord himself should communicate himself to the devout soul, embracing it with love, inciting it to praise of himself, and disposing it for the way which will enable the soul to serve him better in the future. Accordingly, the one giving the Exercises ought...to allow the Creator to deal immediately with the creature and the creature with its Creator and Lord.   —Sp. Ex., #15

Principle and Foundation

Human beings are created to praise, reverence, and serve God our Lord, and by means of this to save their souls. The other things on the face of the earth are created for the human beings, to help them in the pursuit of the end for which they are created. From this it follows that I should use these things to the extent that they help me toward my end, and rid myself of them to the extent that they hinder me.
                                                    —Sp. Ex., #23

Preparation

The Preparatory Prayer is to ask God our Lord for the grace that all my intentions, actions, and operations may be ordered purely to the service and praise of the Divine Majesty.
                                                    —Sp. Ex., #46

A step or two away from the place where I will make my contemplation or meditation, I will stand for the length of an Our Father. I will raise my mind and think how God our Lord is looking at me, and other such thoughts. Then I will make an act of reverence or humility.
                                                    —Sp. Ex., #75

Praying to Christ on the Cross

Imagine Christ our Lord suspended on the cross before you, and converse with him in a colloquy: How is it that he, although he is the Creator, has come to make himself a human being? How is it that he has passed from eternal life to death here in time, and to die in this way for my sins?

In a similar way, reflect on yourself and ask: What have I done for Christ? What am I doing for Christ? What ought I to do for Christ?

—Sp. Ex., #53

Seeking the More (the Magis)

Those who desire to show greater devotion and to distinguish themselves in total service to their eternal King and universal Lord, will not only offer their persons for the labor, but go further still…they will make offerings of greater worth and moment.

—Sp. Ex., #97

Deep Personal Love for Jesus Christ

The third prelude will be to ask for what I desire. Here it will be to ask for an interior knowledge of Our Lord, who became human for me, that I may love him more intensely and follow him more closely.

—Sp. Ex., #104

Contemplation to Attain Love

The second prelude is to ask for what I desire. Here it will be to ask for interior knowledge of all the great good I have received, in order that, stirred to profound gratitude, I may become able to love and serve the Divine majesty in all things.

I will call back into my memory the gifts I have received—my creation, redemption, and other gifts particular to myself. I will ponder with deep affection how much God our Lord has done for me, and how much he has given me of what he possesses....Then I will reflect on myself, and consider what I on my part ought in all reason and justice to offer and give to the Divine Majesty, namely all my possessions, and myself along with them. I will speak as one making an offering with deep affection, and say:

> Take, Lord, and receive all my liberty, my memory, my understanding, and all my will—all that I have and possess. You Lord, have given all that to me. I now give it back to you, O Lord. All of it is yours. Dispose of it according to your will. Give me your love and your grace, for that is enough for me.

—Sp. Ex., #233–34

What I Desire

The second prelude is to ask God our Lord for what I want and desire. What I ask for should be in accordance with the subject matter. For example, in a contemplation of the Resurrection, I will ask for joy with Christ in joy; in a contemplation of the Passion, I will ask for pain, tears, and suffering with Christ suffering.

—Sp. Ex., #48

Colloquy

A colloquy is made, properly speaking, in the way one friend speaks to another, or a servant to one in authority—now begging a favor, now accusing oneself of some misdeed, now telling one's concern and asking counsel about them.

—Sp. Ex., #54

Colloquy for Contemplation on the Incarnation

At the end a colloquy should be made. I will think over what I ought to say to the Three Divine Persons, or to the eternal Word made flesh, or to our Mother and Lady. I will beg favors according to what I perceive in my heart, that I may better follow and imitate Our Lord, who in this way has recently become a human being.

—Sp. Ex., #109

Reflection

After finishing the exercise, for a quarter of an hour, either seated or walking about, I will examine how well I did in the contemplation or meditation. If poorly, I will seek the reasons; and if I find them, I will express sorrow in order to do better in the future. If I did well, I will thank God our Lord and use the same procedure next time.

—Sp. Ex., #77

General Examen
(Examen of Consciousness)

The general examen helps us become more aware of God's activity in our daily lives and more sensitive to the many ways God touches us. It is an important way of seeking and finding God in our daily lives and responding more fully to his loving call. The following steps in making the examen are based on #43 of the Spiritual Exercises.

1. I recall the graces and blessings that have been received this day and I give thanks to God for them.
2. I pray for light and greater insight into the way God has been present to me during the day and the ways I have or have not responded to him.

3. I prayerfully make a review of the day. I seek to become more aware of God's action within me, of the interior movements that may have arisen in me during the course of the day, both the ones that drew me to God and the ones that drew me away from him. I seek to discern and clarify how God has been present to me during the day. Then I reflect on my responses and my actions—the times I have responded to his graces and the times I have failed to do so.
4. I acknowledge my faults and failings and humbly seek God's forgiveness.
5. I resolve with his grace to do better and to go on with renewed hope and trust.

Early Jesuits
Missioned Far and Wide

With the new order's strong emphasis on apostolic works and a generosity in the service of Christ, the early Jesuits were soon traveling to all parts of Europe and to distant places. Tradition has it that St. Ignatius, when he sent St. Francis Xavier to the East, told him, "Ite inflammate omnia" ("Go set the world alight"). Although they were physically separated, they would be united in prayer. This is reflected in the prayer for the whole society of St. Peter Canisius, the great apostle to Germany who did so much to restore the Catholic Church in that country.

Letters played an important role in fostering a spirit of prayer, support, and unity. The more than six thousand letters of St. Ignatius are a major source for his spiritual legacy, and he constantly encouraged the writing of these letters on the part of his companions. The letters of St. Francis Xavier from the East and those from Blessed Peter Faber amid his journeys all over Europe clearly show the value placed on a spirit of mutual prayer.

A deep and abiding love of Jesus Christ and his church provided the motivating force in all the apostolic endeavors. St. Edmund Campion expressed this in his stirring words before his martyrdom at Tyburn in England, and the North American martyrs St. John de Brébeuf and St. Isaac Jogues constantly evoked the name of Jesus in their prayer. It was also the dominant theme in the tender poems of the English priest, poet, and martyr St. Robert Southwell. Perhaps it is said the best in Francis Xavier's simple and direct prayer, "O God I Love You."

Prayer for the Society

I commend to You, Lord Jesus, the entire body of our Society, that it may be properly governed in its superiors and subjects, in the healthy and the sick, in those advancing and those who are lagging behind, in things spiritual and temporal, for the glory of Your name and the good of the whole Church. Through You may we increase in number and excellence all over the world, understand aright our vocation and, understanding, love it and perfectly fulfill its requirements, so that all classes of the Society may worthily and faithfully serve Your divine Majesty, carefully walk the way of the evangelical precepts and counsels, and, united by the bond of brotherly love, experience Thy efficacious blessing in their provinces, colleges, missions, and in the performance of their duties and ministries. May they be sober-minded and simple, prudent, quiet, and intent on the practice of solid virtue, so that their life be in accord with their name, and their profession be renowned by their works.

Confirm, Lord Jesus, what You have begun in Your Society, that, as we made the holy promises of religious obedience, poverty, and chastity under Your inspiration, we may with Your assistance keep them until death. And not only the living but the deceased brethren also of this society, its founders and benefactors, we commend to Your divine Majesty.

—St. Peter Canisius, SJ

A Central Grace

I close, praying that the most holy Trinity by its infinite and supreme goodness may bestow upon all of us plentiful grace to know its most holy will and perfectly to fulfill it.

—Letter of St. Ignatius (1536)

Remembering Ignatius

That year Inigo [Ignatius] entered the same Collège Sainte-Barbe and lodged in the same room as ourselves.... Eternally blessed be all this that divine providence arranged for my good and for my salvation. For after providence decreed that I was to be the instructor of that holy man, we conversed at first about secular matters, then about spiritual things. Then followed a life in common in which we two shared the same room, the same table, and the same purse. As time passed he became my master in spiritual things and gave me a method of raising myself to a knowledge of the divine will and of myself. In the end we became one in desire and will and one in a firm resolve to take up that life we lead today—we, the present or future members of this Society of which I am unworthy.

May it please the divine clemency to give me the grace of clearly remembering and pondering the benefits which the Lord conferred on me in those days through that man.

—Blessed Peter Faber, SJ

Prayer before a Journey

There is nothing more to tell you except that we are about to embark. We close by asking Christ our Lord for the grace of seeing each other joined together in the next life; for I do not know if we shall ever see each other again in this because of the great distance between Rome and India and the great harvest to be found there without going to seek it in another region. Whoever will be the first to go to the other life and does not there find his brother, whom he loves in the Lord, must ask Christ our Lord to unite us all there in his glory.

—Francis Xavier to Ignatius, March 18, 1541

To Know God's Will

I thus bring this to a close, asking your holy Charity, most reverend Father of my soul, as I kneel upon the ground while writing this as if I were in your presence, to commend me much to God our Lord in your holy and devout sacrifices and prayers, so that he may grant me to know his most holy will in this present life and give me the grace to fulfill it perfectly. Amen. And I commend the same to all those of the Society.

—Francis Xavier to Ignatius, January 12, 1549

Farewell to the Novices at Coimbra

And so, my dearest brothers, I write the farewells I would have wished to say. Will this parting be for long? I cannot say....but live happily in Christ and serve the Lord with joy. Never separate yourselves from him who is all our strength. Attach yourselves to no one but Jesus who can never be taken away from you....Only one thing matters: to fix our hearts on him whom God wishes us to follow, Jesus Christ, the mediator between God and man, he who is all in all.

—Blessed Peter Faber, SJ

O Deus Ego Amo Te

O God, I love Thee, I love Thee—
Not out of hope of heaven for me
Nor fearing not to love and be
In the everlasting burning.
Thou, thou, my Jesus, after me
Didst reach Thine arms out dying,
For my sake sufferedst nails and lance,
Mocked and marred countenance,
Sorrows passing number,
Sweat and care and cumber
Yea and death, and this for me,

And Thou couldst see me sinning;
Then I, why should not I love Thee,
Jesus, so much in love with me?
Not for heaven's sake; not to be
Out of hell by loving Thee;
Not for any gains I see;
But just the way that Thou didst me
I do love and I will love Thee:
What must I love Thee, Lord, for then?
For being my king and God. Amen.

—St Francis Xavier (translated by
Gerard Manley Hopkins, SJ)

Discipleship

Then, with great fervor and a totally new awareness, I wished and petitioned that I might at last be allowed to become the servant and the minister of Christ, who consoles, helps, delivers, heals, liberates, saves, enriches, and strengthens. I asked that I also, through him, might be enabled to come to the aid of many, to console them and free them from many ills, to deliver and strengthen them, to bring them light not in spiritual matters alone but also (if I may be allowed the boldness of presuming it in God) in a material way, together with whatever charity can do for the soul and body of any of my fellowmen.

—Blessed Peter Faber, SJ

On Friendship

Matteo Ricci (1552–1610) was the great apostle to China. On Friendship, written at the request of a Chinese prince, was the first book he wrote in Chinese. Translated excerpts follow:

Before making friends, we should scrutinize. After making friends, we should trust.

When life is peaceful and without trouble, it is difficult to distinguish the true from the false friend. Only when difficulties arise do the true feelings of a friend reveal themselves. For in a time of crisis, true friends will draw closer, and false friends will become increasingly scarce.

Whoever makes friends thinking only of personal profit without also considering the benefit of a friend is nothing more than a merchant, and cannot be called a friend.

I think without sadness about friends who have died, for when they were alive I held them as if I could lose them. And now that they have passed away, I think about them as if they were still alive.

Someone who comes to see me in my hour of glory only when invited, and who comes to see me in my hour of trouble even when not invited—now *that* is a friend.

If you cannot be a friend to yourself, how can you be a friend to another?

In ancient times, there were two men walking together, one who was extremely rich, and one who was extremely poor. Someone commented: "Those two men have become very close friends." Hearing this, Dou-fade (a famous sage of antiquity) retorted: "If that is indeed so, why is it that one of them is rich and other poor?"

❖

Once upon a time, there was a man who asked a friend to do something unethical, but when the friend refused, he said, "If you will not agree to do what I ask, what good are you as a friend?" To which the other replied: "If you ask me to do what is unethical, what good are *you* as a friend?"

A Principle of Action

Nothing is too arduous that has for its purpose the honor of God and the salvation of souls.

—Blessed Joseph de Anchieta, SJ (Apostle of Brazil)

Before Martyrdom

It was not our death that ever we feared. But we knew that we were not lords of our own lives, and therefore for want of answer would not be guilty of our deaths. The only thing that we have now to say is, that if our religion do make us traitors, we are worthy to be condemned; but otherwise are, and have been, as good subjects as ever the Queen had.

In condemning us you condemn all your own ancestors—all the ancient priests, bishops and kings—all that was once the glory of England, the island of saints, and the most devoted child of the See of Peter.

For what have we taught, however you may qualify it with the odious name of treason, that they did not uniformly teach? To be condemned with these lights—not of England only, but of the world—by their degenerate descendants, is both gladness and glory to us.

God lives; posterity will live; their judgment is not so liable to corruption as that of those who are now going to sentence us to death.

—St. Edmund Campion, SJ (1581)

A Child My Choice

Let folly praise that fancy loves, I praise and love
    that child
Whose heart no thought, whose tongue no word,
    whose hand no deed defiled.
I praise him most, I love him best, all praise and love
    is his;
While him I love, in him I live, and cannot live amiss.

Love's sweetest mark, laud's highest theme, man's
    most desired light,
To love him life, to leave him death, to live in him
    delight.
He mine by gift, I his by debt, thus each to other due.
First friend he was, best friend he is, all times will try
    him true.

Though young, yet wise, though small, yet strong;
    though man, yet God he is;
As wise, he knows, as strong he can, as God he loves
    to bless.
His knowledge rules, his strength defends, his love
    doth cherish all;
His birth our joy, his life our light, his death our end
    of thrall.

Alas! He weeps, he sighs, he pants, yet do His angels
    sing;
Out of his tears, his sighs and throbs, doth bud a
    joyful spring.
Almighty Babe, whose tender arms can force all foes
    to fly,
Correct my faults, protect my life, direct me when I
    die.

—St. Robert Southwell, SJ

The Burning Babe

As I in hoary winter's night stood shivering in the
    snow,
Surprised I was with sudden heat which made my
    heart to glow;
And lifting up a fearful eye to view what fire was near,
A pretty babe all burning bright did in the air appear;
Who, scorchèd with excessive heat, such floods of
    tears did shed,
As though His floods should quench His flames,
    which with His tears were fed.
"Alas!" quoth He, "but newly born in fiery heats I fry,
Yet none approach to warm their hearts or feel my
    fire but I!

My faultless breast the furnace is, the fuel wounding
    thorns,
Love is the fire, and sighs the smoke, the ashes shame
    and scorns;
The fuel Justice layeth on, and Mercy blows the coals,
The metal in this furnace wrought are men's defiled
    souls,
For which, as now on fire I am to work them to their
    good,
So will I melt into a bath to wash them in my blood."
With this he vanished out of sight and swiftly shrunk
    away,
And straight I callèd unto mind that it was
    Christmas day.

—St. Robert Southwell, SJ

St. Robert Southwell, SJ (1561–95) was hanged, drawn, and quartered for the crime of being a Catholic priest in post-Reformation England.

What Return Shall I Make

Jesus, my Lord and Savior, what can I give you in return for all the favors you have conferred on me? I *will take* from your hand *the cup* of your sufferings and *call on your name*. I vow before your eternal Father and the Holy Spirit, before your most holy Mother and her most chaste spouse, before the angels, apostles and martyrs, before my blessed fathers, Saint Ignatius and Saint Francis Xavier—in truth I vow to you, Jesus my Savior, that as far as I have the strength I will never fail to accept the grace of martyrdom, if some day you in your infinite mercy should offer it to me, your most unworthy servant.

—St. John de Brébeuf, SJ

A Martyr's Heroic Death: St. René Goupil

One day, then, as in the grief of our souls we had gone forth from the Village, in order to pray more suitably and with less disturbance, two young men came after us to tell us that we must return home. I had some presentiment of what was to happen, and said to him: "My dearest brother, let us commend ourselves to Our Lord and to our good mother the blessed Virgin; these people have some evil design as I think." We had offered ourselves to Our Lord, shortly before, with much devotion—beseeching him to receive our lives and our blood, and to unite them with his life and his blood for the salvation of these poor peoples. We accordingly return toward the Village, reciting our rosary, of which we had already said 4 decades. Having stopped near the gate of the Village, to see what they might say to us, one of those two Iroquois draws a hatchet, which he held concealed under his blanket, and deals a blow with it on the head of René, who was before him. He falls motionless, his face to the ground, pronouncing the holy name of JESUS (often we admonished each other that this holy name should end both our voices and our lives).

—St. Isaac Jogues, SJ

The North American Martyrs came from France to evangelize the Hurons in upstate New York and Canada and were martyred in the mid-seventeenth century. They included St. Isaac Jogues, SJ, St. John de Brébeuf, SJ, and St. René Goupil, SJ.

The Two Poles of All Spirituality

The two elements of the spiritual life are the cleansing of the heart and the direction of the Holy Spirit. These are the two poles of all spirituality. By these two ways we arrive at perfection according to the degree of purity we have attained, and in proportion to the fidelity with which we have cooperated with the movements of the Holy Spirit and followed his guidance.

—Louis Lallemant, SJ (1588–1635)

The Guidance of the Holy Spirit

We have a figure of the guidance of the Holy Spirit in that which God adopted in regard to the Israelites in their exodus from Egypt during their journeying in the wilderness towards the land of promise. He gave them as their guide a pillar of cloud by day, and a pillar of fire by night. They followed the movements of this pillar, and halted when it halted; they did not go before it, they only followed it, and never wandered from it. It is thus we ought to act with respect to the Holy Spirit.

—Louis Lallemant, SJ

A Spirit of Hope

We must hope and expect great things from God, because the merits of our Lord belong to us; and to hope much in God is to honour him much. The more we hope, the more we honour him.

—Louis Lallemant, SJ

The Present Moment

What was the best thing for us to do in the moment that has passed is no longer so, for the will of God is now manifesting itself in those circumstances which are the duty of the present moment. It is the fulfilling of this duty, no matter in what guise it presents itself, which does most to make one holy.

—Jean-Pierre de Caussade, SJ

God's Will

If we do not concentrate entirely on doing the will of God we shall find neither happiness nor holiness, no matter what pious practices we adopt, however excellent they may be. If you are not satisfied with what God chooses for you, what else can please you?…In reality, nothing benefits us that does not arise from God's will, and there is absolutely nothing that gives us more peace or does more to make us holy than obeying the will of God.

—Jean-Pierre de Caussade, SJ

A New Heart

O God, what will You do to conquer the fearful hardness of our hearts? Lord, You must give us new hearts, tender hearts, sensitive hearts, to replace hearts that are made of marble and of bronze.

You must give us your own Heart, Jesus. Come, lovable Heart of Jesus. Place Your Heart deep in the center of our hearts and enkindle in each heart a flame of love as strong, as great, as the sum of all the reasons that I have for loving You, my God.

O holy Heart of Jesus, dwell hidden in my heart, so that I may live only in You and only for You, so that, in the end, I may live with You eternally in heaven.

—St. Claude la Columbière, SJ

Perfect Confidence

My God, I believe most firmly that You watch over all who hope in You, and that we can want for nothing when we rely upon You in all things; therefore I am resolved for the future to have no anxieties and to cast all my cares upon You. "In peace in the selfsame I will sleep and I will rest; for you, O Lord, singularly have settled me in hope."

—St. Claude la Columbière, SJ

True Devotion

The principle of devotion is, that God being the one source and the one author of holiness, the reasonable creature ought to depend on Him in everything, and be absolutely governed by the Spirit of God. We must be always attached to God in the depths of our souls, always attentive to His voice within us, always faithful to accomplish what He asks of us each moment.

—Jean Nicolas Grou, SJ

Come, O Divine Spirit

Come, O divine Spirit! Come and dwell and act within me. Take entire possession of my understanding and my will; direct their exercise not alone at the time of prayer, but at all times. I can neither glorify God, nor sanctify my soul without Thee. Amen.

—Jean Nicolas Grou, SJ

Later Jesuits

*United in Prayer and
Apostolic Service*

Later Jesuits continued to carry out the vision of St. Ignatius in a great variety of apostolic endeavors in changed circumstances and facing new challenges. Among them are numbered saints and martyrs, missionaries, educators, scientists, preachers, theologians, and various pastoral and retreat ministers.

It should be kept in mind that Ignatius's vision calls not only for an active person and one totally committed to his apostolic work, but for a person who brings a strong and abiding contemplative dimension to that work. "Finding God in all things" and being "a contemplative in action" are the traditional mottoes for this essential orientation. This has been expressed in a special way in the rich imagery of the poet Gerard Manley Hopkins (1844–89) and the mystic eye of the paleontologist Teilhard de Chardin (1881–1955).

God's Grandeur

The world is charged with the grandeur of God.
    It will flame out, like shining from shook foil;
    It gathers to a greatness, like the ooze of oil
Crushed. Why do men then now not reck his rod?
Generations have trod, have trod, have trod;
    And all is seared with trade; bleared, smeared
        with toil;
    And wears man's smudge, and shares man's
        smell: the soil
Is bare now, nor can foot feel, being shod.

And for all this, nature is never spent;
> There lives the dearest freshness deep down
>> things;
And though the last light off the black West went
> Oh, morning, at the brown brink eastward,
>> springs—
Because the Holy Ghost over the bent
> World broods with warm breast and with ah!
>> Bright wings.
>>> —Gerard Manley Hopkins, SJ

Hurrahing in Harvest

Summer ends now; now barbarous in beauty, the
> stooks rise
Around; up above, what wind-walks! what lovely
> behaviour
Of silk-sacked clouds! Has wilder, willful-wavier
Meal-drift moulded ever and melted across skies?

I walk, I lift up, I lift up heart, eyes,
Down all that glory in the heavens to glean our
> Saviour;
And, eyes, heart, what looks, what lips yet gave you a
Rapturous love's greeting of realer, of rounder replies?

And the azurous hung hills are his world-wielding
> shoulder
Majestic—as a stallion stalwart, very-violet-sweet!—
These things, these things were here and but the
> beholder
Wanting; which two when they once meet,
The heart rears wings bold and bolder
And hurls for him, O half hurls earth for him off
> under his feet.
>> —Gerard Manley Hopkins, SJ

Pied Beauty

Glory be God for dappled things—
  For skies of couple-colour as a brinded cow;
    For rose-moles all in stipple upon trout that
      swim;
Fresh-firecoal chestnut-falls; finches' wings;
  Landscape plotted and pieced—fold, fallow, and
    plough;
    And all trades, their gear and tackle and trim

All things counter, original, spare, strange;
  Whatever is fickle, freckled (who knows how?)
    With swift, slow; sweet, sour; adazzle, dim;
He fathers-forth whose beauty is past change:
  Praise him.
                              —Gerard Manley Hopkins, SJ

As Kingfishers Catch Fire

As kingfishers catch fire, dragonflies dráw flame;
As tumbled over rim in roundy wells
Stones ring; like each tucked string tells, each hung bell's
Bow swung finds tongue to fling out broad its name;
Each mortal thing does one thing and the same;
Deals out that being indoors each one dwells;
Selves—goes its self; *myself* it speaks and spells;
Crying *Whát I dó is me: for that I came.*

Í say móre: the just man justices;
Kéeps gráce: thát keeps all his goings graces;
Acts in God's eyes what in God's eye he is—
Chríst—for Christ plays in ten thousand places,
Lovely in limbs, and lovely in eyes not his
To the Father through the features of men's faces.
                              —Gerard Manley Hopkins, SJ

Lord of the World

Lord Jesus Christ, you truly contain within your gentleness, within your humanity, all the unyielding immensity and grandeur of the world.

You are the Center at which all things meet and which stretches out over all things so as to draw them back into itself; I love you for the extensions of your body and soul to the farthest corners of creation through grace, through life, and through matter.

Lord Jesus, you who are as gentle as the human heart, as fiery as the forces of nature, as intimate as life itself, you in whom I can melt away and with whom I must have mastery and freedom; I love you as a world, as *this* world which has captivated my heart....

Lord Jesus, you are the center towards which all things are moving.

—Pierre Teilhard de Chardin, SJ

Priestly Prayer

To the full extent of my power, *because I am a priest*, I wish from now on to be the first to become conscious of all that the world loves, pursues and suffers; I want to be the first to seek, to sympathise and to suffer; the first to open myself out and sacrifice myself—to become more widely human and more nobly of the earth than any of the world's servants....

I feel so weak, Lord, that I hardly dare ask you to let me participate in that beatitude. But I perceive it clearly enough, and I proclaim: Happy are those of us who, in these decisive days of the Creation and the Redemption, are chosen for this supreme act, the logical crowning of their priesthood: communion unto death with Christ.

—Pierre Teilhard de Chardin, SJ

The Mass on the World

Since once again, Lord—though this time not in the forests of the Aisne but in the steppes of Asia—I have neither bread, nor wine, nor altar, I will raise myself beyond these symbols, up to the pure majesty of the real itself; I, your priest, will make the whole earth my altar and on it will offer you all the labours and sufferings of the world.

—Pierre Teilhard de Chardin, SJ

Saviour of Human Activity

Jesus, Saviour of human activity to which you have given meaning, Saviour of human suffering to which you have given living value, be also the Saviour of human unity; compel us to discard our pettiness, and to venture forth, resting upon you, into the uncharted ocean of charity.

—Pierre Teilhard de Chardin, SJ

Immersed in God

To repeat by virtue of the Creation and, still more, of the Incarnation, nothing here below is profane for those who know how to see. On the contrary, everything is sacred to the men who can distinguish that portion of chosen being which is subject to Christ's drawing power in the process of consummation. Try, with God's help, to perceive the connection—even physical and natural—which binds your labour with the building of the kingdom of heaven; try to realize that heaven itself smiles upon you and, through your works, draws you to itself; then, as you leave church for the noisy streets, you will remain with only one feeling, that of continuing to immerse yourself in God.

—Pierre Teilhard de Chardin, SJ

Light for the Road

Let your light be for me like the burning bush for Moses, the light of Damascus for Paul, the Cardoner and La Storta for Ignatius. That is, a call to set out on a road that may be obscure, but that will open up before me, as happened to Ignatius when he was following it.

—Pedro Arrupe, SJ (1907–91)

Finding God

Nothing is more practical than finding God, that is, than falling in love in a quite absolute, final way. What you are in love with, what seizes your imagination, will affect everything. It will decide what will get you out of bed in the morning, what you will do with your evenings, how you spend your weekend, what you read, what you know, what breaks your heart, and what amazes you with joy and gratitude. Fall in love, stay in love, and it will decide everything.

—Pedro Arrupe, SJ

Being-in-Love

You may ask whether ordinary human beings ever seriously and perseveringly transcend themselves. I think they do so when they fall in love. Then their being becomes being-in-love. Such being-in-love has its antecedents, its causes, its conditions, its occasions. But once it has occurred and as long as it lasts, it takes over. It becomes the first principle. From it flow one's desires and fears, one's joys and sorrows, one's discernment of values, one's vision of possibilities, one's decisions and deeds.

—Bernard Lonergan, SJ

God's Gift of Love

God's gift of his love to us is the crowning point of our self-transcendence. St. Augustine wrote: "Thou hast made us for thyself, O Lord, and our hearts are restless till they rest in thee." But that resting in God is something, not that we achieve, but that we receive, accept, ratify. It comes quietly, secretly, unobtrusively. We know about it when we notice its fruits in our lives. It is the profoundest fulfillment of the human spirit. Because it is fulfillment, it gives us peace, the peace that the world cannot give. Because it is fulfillment, it gives us joy, a joy that can endure despite the sorrows of failure, humiliation, privation, pain, betrayal, desertion.

—Bernard Lonergan, SJ

Only in Love

Only in love can I find You, my God. In love the gates of my soul spring open, allowing me to breathe a new air of freedom and forget my own petty self. In love my whole being streams forth out of the rigid confines of narrowness and anxious self-assertion, which makes me a prisoner of my own poverty and emptiness. In love all the powers of my soul flow out toward You, wanting never more to return, but to lose themselves completely in You, since by Your love you are the inmost center of my heart, closer to me than I am to myself.

—Karl Rahner, SJ

You Alone

May You alone enlighten me, You alone speak to me. May all that I know apart from You be nothing more than a chance traveling companion on the journey toward You. May it help to mature me, so that I may ever better understand You in the suffering that it brings me, as Your holy writer has predicted. When it has accomplished this, then it can quietly disappear into oblivion.

—Karl Rahner, SJ

Inner Self

Be merciful to me, my God. When I flee from prayer, it's not that I want to flee from You, but from myself and my own superficiality. I don't want to run away from Your Infinity and Holiness, but from the deserted marketplace of my own soul. Every time I pray, I am doomed to wander in the barren wastes of my own emptiness, since I have left the world behind, and still cannot find my way into the true sanctuary of my inner self, the only place where You can be found and adored.

—Karl Rahner, SJ

Waiting

Give me, O God of my prayer, the grace to continue waiting for You in prayer.

—Karl Rahner, SJ

Sacrament of Eternal Life

Lord of eternal glory, may we always be ready, full of faith and courage, to enter into Your eternal life. When we receive You, may Your body be to us the pledge of eternal glory. O Sacrament of Eternal Life, grant that we may be given our heart's last desire: to see You at last face to face and to adore You with the Father and the Holy Spirit for ever. Amen.

—Karl Rahner, SJ

The Mystery of the Church

That voice of Tradition has continually called on me to look up into the "Heavenly Jerusalem" whose beauty has taken a daily firmer hold upon me. But for all that I have not looked to the heavenly city as one does to a dream; for I have not been looking for a sort of refuge from everyday monotony and the burden of existence, in some airy mirage or other. On the contrary; to me, that mother-country of freedom, with all its royal majesty and heavenly splendor, is something to be seen at the very heart of earthly reality, right at the core of all the confusion and all the mischances which are, inevitably, involved in its mission to men. My love is for the Holy city not only as it is ideally, but also as it appears in history, and particularly as it appears to us at present; and I love it with an ever-growing affection. So, since that is where my heart lies, and since heart speaks to heart, my hope is that others—especially my fellow priests—will find helpful what has been of help to me.

—Henri de Lubac, SJ (1896–1991)

Meditation: Eastern Point Retreat House

This is a place to fall in love again
Those voices in the wind
    We've heard before;
The psalms of David shout
    And say, AMEN
The Spirit weeps at our October door.

This is a place where the Gloucester sea
Bangs my heart like dolphins, God
    Dives me deep;
He bindeth me with weeds—
Soaked and salted, I am cod.

O fabled, Christian fish of old,
    Leviathan or minnow, great and small,
Swim the troubled waters of my soul,
    Take my bait, be my haul.

Riding easy down this summer bay—
    Do not be the one that got away.

—Leonard J. McCarthy, SJ

At the Beginning of the Day

O God, I find myself at the beginning of another day. I do not know what it will bring. Please help me to be ready for whatever it may be. If I am to stand up, help me to stand bravely. If I am to sit still, help me to sit quietly. If I am to lie low, help me to do it patiently. If I am to do nothing, let me do it gallantly. I pray just for today, for these twenty-four hours, for the ability to cooperate with others according to the way Jesus taught us to live. "Your kingdom come, your will be done on earth as it is in heaven." May these words that he taught us become more than words. Please free my thinking and feelings and the thinking and feelings of others, from all forms of self-will, self-centeredness, dishonesty, and deception. Along with my brothers and sisters, I need this freedom to make my choices today according to your desires. Send your Spirit to inspire us in time of doubt and indecision so that, together, we can walk along your path. Amen.

—Adapted from an unknown source by John Veltri, SJ
(1933–2008)

Jesus, Love of My Heart

Jesus, love of my heart, my peace my life,
When shall I see you in the streets of heaven?

I melt like a candle starred with that burning hope—
To turn and find you standing at my side.

The lovely thought, so precious to my mind,
Paints on my heart your Face like a die of gold;

And happier run the hours while I read,
Your love my book, your wounds its printed page.

—Francis W. Sweeney, SJ (1916–2002)
(from the Italian of Bernardine Realino, SJ [d. 1616])

Patient Trust

Above all, trust in the slow work of God. We are quite naturally impatient in everything to reach the end without delay. We should like to skip the intermediate stages; we are impatient of being on the way to something unknown, something new. And yet it is the law of all progress that it is made by passing through some stages of instability—and that it may take a very long time. And so I think it is with you, your ideas mature gradually—let them grow, let them shape themselves, without undue haste. Don't try to force them on, as though you could be today what time (that is to say, grace and circumstances acting on your own good will) will make of you tomorrow. Only God could say what this new spirit gradually forming within you will be. Give Our Lord the benefit of believing that his hand is leading you, and accept the anxiety of feeling yourself in suspense and incomplete.

—Pierre Teilhard de Chardin, SJ

Conversion

That night, for the first time in years, I prayed. I knelt down in the chill blackness at my bedside, as my mother had taught me to do when I was a little boy, and attempted to raise my heart and mind toward Him of Whose presence and power I had become so unexpectedly aware. I recited the Our Father. The words came slowly, and I had to make many new starts before the whole prayer unfolded itself in my mind. Our Father Who art in Heaven. Hallowed be Thy name. Thy will be done on earth, as it is in heaven....

—Avery Dulles, SJ (1918–2008)

His Grace Will Not Fail Me

If the Kingdom is the pearl of great price, the treasure buried in the field, one should be prepared to give up everything else to acquire it. It has always seemed to me that if

God is God, his honor and glory must be the first priority. Although I cannot rival the generous dedication of Sts. Paul and Ignatius of Loyola, I am, like them, content to be employed in the service of Christ and the gospel, whether in sickness or in health, in good repute or ill repute. I am immeasurably grateful for the years in which the Lord has permitted me to serve him in a society that bears as its motto: *Ad majorem Dei gloriam*. I trust that his grace will not fail me, and that I will not fail his grace, in the years to come.

—Avery Dulles, SJ

You Shape Me

Lord, mighty God, in power and wisdom You shape me and my world. You choose my life world—my time, my city, my language. You give me understanding and passions; You fill me with desiring and with energies. You give me voice to sing songs to You for all creation. For all that has passed between us, I thank You. To all that You are now doing in me, I say yes. In the name of Him in whom everything says yes, Jesus, my Lord and good brother, who lives and reigns with you, forever and ever. Amen.

—Joseph Tetlow, SJ

Lord of Life

Lord Jesus Christ,
You have yearned to heal every one of us
from all our withered hands and spirits.
You are the Lord of Life, of the living,
and where You go, there is life to its full.
Lord, I would go with You,
and when I fear that I do not know where You go
and do not know the way,
heal me then and fill me with Your courage.

—Joseph Tetlow, SJ

Our Guide

We speak of you as our Guide, dear Lord. But you are so much else. You are the one who put Life above law, and Love above life. You were not nearly so much the Law-giver as the one who exemplified all the brightness and inner glow and freedom and richness of the law well observed. You were the one who showed that the law is not in the mind but in the heart; not in books but in personal conduct. You were the Ruler of the world, yet you reduced all rules to the simple rule of Love.

Let me see through your eyes and imitate the gestures of your hands, love those you love and pity those you pity, hate the things you hate, and overcome, not with force but with the power of your personal conduct, the evil of the world.

—Daniel A. Lord, SJ (1888–1955)

My God, You Depend Upon Me

In the dimness of my constant failures, I am simply baffled by the fact that you still permit yourself to depend upon me. But you do, dear Lord; you do. You give me all the graces necessary to be a saint. But you will not force sainthood on me. Whether or not I am a saint depends upon my use of your gifts....

Often in retreats to others I have said what must be one of the great platitudes: "God has given you a place in his plan. If you fulfill it, he will be pleased and his plan will be perfected. If you fail him, there is nothing that even God can do about it." Then, you remember, at great length I have talked of how you depend upon each of us and all of us, the greatest and the smallest. It was easy to say that to others because it is transparently true. Now I say it to myself, and I am afraid.

My God, you depend upon me.

—Daniel A. Lord, SJ

God's Will

Now, with sudden and almost blinding clarity and simplicity, I realized I had been trying to do something with my own will and intellect that was at once too much and mostly all wrong. God's will was not hidden somewhere "out there" in the situations in which I found myself; the situations themselves were his will for me. What he wanted was for me to accept these situations as from his hands, to let go of the reins and place myself entirely at his disposal.

—Walter Ciszek, SJ (1904–84)

Prayer of Surrender

Lord, Jesus Christ, I ask the grace to accept the sadness in my heart, as your will for me, in this moment. I offer it up, in union with your sufferings, for those who are in deepest need of your redeeming grace. I surrender myself to your Father's will, and I ask you to help me to move on to the next task that you have set for me.

Spirit of Christ, help me to enter into a deeper union with you. Lead me away from dwelling on the hurt I feel: to thoughts of charity for those who need my love, to thoughts of compassion for those who need my care, and to thoughts of giving to those who need my help

As I give myself to you, help me to provide for the salvation of those who come to me in need. May I find my healing in this giving. May I always accept God's will. May I find my true self by living for others in a spirit of sacrifice and suffering. May I die more fully to myself, and live more fully in you.

As I seek to surrender to the Father's will, may I come to trust that he will do everything for me.

—Adapted from the spiritual teaching of
Walter J. Ciszek, SJ

My Spirituality

So then, should anyone ask what I understand by spirituality, my basic response would be: My spirituality is my Christian living as guided by the Holy Spirit. Not some ghostly apparition in outer space, but the Third Person of the Trinity, the divine Person given me by the Father and the Son, alive within me, shaping me into an image of Christ, shaping me increasingly as brother in Christ to all who are children of the Father. How does the Holy Spirit effect this? By infusing into me incredible gifts that I could not possibly produce by my naked human nature. I mean a faith which at its best is not only or primarily an acceptance of revealed propositions but a total self-giving to God; a hope which is not a gossamer optimism, but a confident trust in the promises of a God ever faithful; a love which enables me to love my sisters and brothers as Jesus has loved me (1 Cor 13:13).
—Walter J. Burghardt, SJ (1914–2008)

One Life in Christ

The goal of the spiritual life is to allow the Spirit of Christ to influence all our activity, prayer as well as service. Our role in this process is to provide conditions in our lives to enable us to live in tune with his Spirit. Our effort is not a self-conscious striving to fill ourselves with the important Christian virtues; it is more getting out of the way and allowing his spirit to transform all our activities. Christ will do the rest. His Spirit has joined ours and will never abandon us. Gradually we become more and more sensitive to the movements of Christ's spirit in our own hearts; simultaneously we grow in sensitivity to the movement of his Spirit in others. Subtly our vision of the world changes. We begin seeing everything in relationship to Christ and the Father, and so we carry on a continual dialogue with them. Without really trying, we find ourselves fulfilling Paul's injunction to the Ephesians to "Pray always."

—Richard J. Hauser, SJ

John the Baptizer

I sat on a rock this afternoon,
Trying to gather back my thoughts,
Wondering where they all went,
And imagining that John the Baptist
Sat beside me on the shore.

And there we were, weary
In the familiar wilderness
With plenty of crooked paths
That needed straightening,
And the sound of John's voice,
Now two thousand years old,
Still echoing around us.

And I wondered aloud if he was sad
To see his disciples leave
And follow someone else,
Or if his voice was hoarse from shouting
And not being heard,
Or if there wasn't just a pang of regret
When the heavens opened up
And he knew for sure
That it wasn't him God had chosen.

He just looked at me in response,
With the weariness of the wilderness
Showing all around him
And a fire still caught in his eyes
A passion still burning
For crooked ways made straight.

And I realized, for the thousandth time,
That it was never going to be me
For whom the crooked ways became straight
And that it wasn't my love that made John hoarse.

But I left the ghost of the Baptist
With a fire caught in my eyes—
Baptized by his love.

—Thomas Flowers, SJ

Her Name

There's a lot I don't know
About courage.
I think I would have been hiding with the rest,
Or alone, crying

She was crying too,
Just three days after he died,
As she came to the tomb
To tend to the only needs of his
There were left to tend to.
And when she found him gone
It was too much,
And all she wanted to do
Was to find him,
And cling to what was left
Of her life.

She must have heard him
Say it so many times,
And maybe it always made
Her think of the first time
He had spoken her name
And driven out the demons,
When he had saved her
And changed everything.

So maybe the others could hide,
But she had to be near him,
She had to care for him even if it was too late.
And then she heard, "Mary,"
Her name, in his voice,
And it was unmistakable,
And it wasn't too late:
His voice could still calm storms
And shatter hearts of stone
And cast out every demon
Of fear and loneliness from her heart.

She heard him say her name that day
And had the courage
To let him change her life again.

—Thomas Flowers, SJ

Meditation at the Foot of the Cross

What I would ask—because the word "demand" sounds too strong—involves two things. First, that you look with your eyes and heart at these peoples who are suffering so much—some from poverty and hunger, others from oppression and repression. Then, because I am a Jesuit, I would bid you pray the colloquy of St. Ignatius from the first week of the Exercises before this crucified people, asking yourself: What have I done to crucify them? What am I doing to end their crucifixion? What should I do so that this people might rise from the dead?

—Ignacio Ellacuría, SJ (1930–89)

The Christian Journey

The life of Christ is the central metaphor for the Christian life. And the way that Jesus understood who he was, what he was meant to do, and how he was meant to do it, is a metaphor for the Christian journey to the true self. All of us are called to meditate deeply on our own true selves, to embrace the reality of our vocations, and to let God transform our true selves into sources of new life for others. It's a long route, a lifetime journey, but we are not alone. We have the support of the rest of the community, we have the Holy Spirit inspiring us, we have the love of God the Father, and we have the companionship of the truest self of all, Jesus Christ.

—James Martin, SJ

The Call to Holiness

God's invitation to live out our individual vocations is part of what makes the world so marvelously rich. "How gloriously different are the saints!" wrote the English writer C. S. Lewis. The problem comes when we begin to believe that we have to be someone *else* to be holy. We use someone else's map to heaven when God has already planted in our soul all the directions we need. In that way, we ignore our own call to sanctity. When admirers used to visit Calcutta to see Mother Teresa, she would tell many of them, "Find your own Calcutta." In other words, bloom where you are planted. Discover sanctity in your own life.

—James Martin, SJ

Ignatius in the Holy Land (a song)

At last I kissed the holy ground;
I walked where he walked his winding way;
At last the holy city shone
In bright late sunshine, in evening's calm.
Holy the land where he lived, where he trod;
Holy the ground he touched—
Lord let me walk in your winding way;
Let me Lord Jesus walk your way.

Let me touch each tree and rock
Where Jesus walked once, where Jesus prayed.
Let me climb each mountainside
Where Jesus spoke once, where Jesus trod.
Holy the land where he died, where he rose;
Holy the tree he touched—
Lord, let me linger, Lord, let me stay;
Let me Lord Jesus live your way.

—William Hewett, SJ

A Conscious Relationship with God

So your interest in prayer must delight God. I hope that you will give him even more delight by allowing the relationship to develop and deepen. Prayer, after all, is just conscious relationship with God, and like any other conscious relationship this one too grows through mutual revelation or developing transparency. In the process of getting to know God better, I trust that you, too, will come to realize at deeper and deeper levels that God is a lot better than he's made out to be.

—William A. Barry, SJ

The Primary Motive

Yes, prayer does have an effect on the person who prays. But that effect is not the primary motive for praying. It is a by-product. The primary motive for prayer is love, first the love of God for us and then the arousal of our love for God.

—William A. Barry, SJ

A Love that Stretches

Yes, love—true, genuine personal love—always makes a difference. It stretches, invigorates, and challenges our soul. This stretching snaps complacency, calms the undertow of sadness, and lays bare in daily life a glorious freedom. But, as mentioned in the beginning, the heart's desire is limitless. So our longing for love can never settle, finally, for the experience of some limited, finite human love. Implied in these valuable finite experiences is another love beyond all earthly imaging. The revelation of God in the beauty of the risen Jesus adds profound, inexpressible significance to all limited human loving—and lures us on in our inherent thirst for the fullness of love. Jesus himself knew that thirst for love and found it satisfied in the Beloved of his heart, that One who enriched daily life and saw him through its trials and tribulations, its joys and pleasures.

—George A. Aschenbrenner, SJ

I Love Your Promise/Psalm 119

A double heart be far from me, Lord
I love your commands
My hope is your promise

A lying tongue be far from me
I love your promise
My hope is your law

Far from me a violent will
Your will is my hope
I love your commands

To witness your law
To love your commands
Be my first love.

—Daniel Berrigan, SJ

Special Devotions

Among devotions that have a special significance in Jesuit history and practice, three can be highlighted: devotion to the Sacred Heart of Jesus; devotion to Our Lady; and the Novena in honor of St. Francis Xavier.

Devotion to the Sacred Heart of Jesus

Two saints of the seventeenth century did much to foster devotion to the Sacred Heart of Jesus, the Visitandine sister St. Margaret Mary Alacoque and the Jesuit priest Fr. Claude La Columbière. They were the instruments of God for awakening the church to a renewed awareness of God's love symbolized by the heart of Jesus. Since that time there has been a close connection between the Society of Jesus and this devotion, a relationship that has developed over the course of the Society's history, been accepted by the Society "as a most pleasing mission" (munus suavissimum) *and confirmed by various general congregations of the Society.*

Offering to the Sacred Heart

Sacred Heart of Jesus, teach me perfect forgetfulness of self, since this is the only way to find entrance into you. As all I shall do belongs to you, grant that nothing I do be unworthy of you. Teach me what I must do to come to the purity of your love, in fulfillment of the desire you yourself have inspired in me. I have a great will to please you but an even greater inability to do so without the special light and help which I can only hope for from you.

Lord, do your will in me. I am well aware that I oppose it, even though I wish not to. It is yours to do, Divine Heart of Jesus Christ. To you alone the glory of my sanctification, if indeed I do become holy—this is as clear as day to me. But it would be a great glory for you, and this is the only reason I wish to perfect myself. Amen.

—St. Claude La Columbière, SJ

Confirmed in Prayer

Finally, my Saviour, I seemed to be gazing at the heart of your Sacred Body with my own eyes. It was as if you opened it to me and told me to drink from it as from a spring, inviting me to draw the waters of salvation from these springs of yours. I was filled with longing that the waters of faith, hope and charity should flow from your heart into me.

—St. Peter Canisius, SJ

Look upon His Heart

Grant, O Infinite God, that I may ever cling fast to Jesus Christ, my Lord. Let His heart reveal to me how You are disposed toward me. I shall look upon His heart when I desire to know Who you are. The eye of my mind is blinded whenever it looks only at Your infinity, in which You are totally present in each and every aspect at once. Then I am surrounded by the darkness of Your unboundedness, which is harsher than all my earthly nights. But instead I shall gaze upon His human heart, O God of Our Lord Jesus Christ, and then I shall be sure that You love me.

But I have still one more request. Make my heart like that of Your Son. Make it as great and rich in love as His, so that my brothers—or at least one of them, sometime in my life—can enter through this door and there learn that You love him. God of Our Lord Jesus Christ, let me find You in His heart.

—Karl Rahner, SJ

Rooted in Love

From my noviceship on, I have always been convinced that in the so-called devotion to the Sacred Heart there is summed up a symbolic expression of the very core of the Ignatian spirit and extraordinary power—"ultra quam speraverint"—both for personal perfection and for apostolic fruitfulness. This conviction is still mine today.

—Pedro Arrupe, SJ

Heart of Jesus

I believe, O Lord, but strengthen my faith.

Heart of Jesus, I love Thee; but increase my love.

Heart of Jesus, I trust in Thee; but give greater vigor to my confidence.

Heart of Jesus, I give my heart to Thee; but so enclose it in Thee that it may never be separated from Thee.

Heart of Jesus, I am all Thine; but take care of my promise so that I may be able to put it in practice even unto the complete sacrifice of my life.

—Blessed Miguel Pro, SJ (1891–1927)

Apostleship of Prayer

Since its beginnings in 1844, the Apostleship of Prayer has been happily linked with the Devotion to the Sacred Heart and instrumental in fostering and furthering its growth. Central to the Apostleship of Prayer has been its members' recitation of the morning offering. The mission statement of the Apostleship of Prayer reads: "The mission of the Apostleship of Prayer is to encourage Christians to make a daily offering of themselves to the Lord for the coming of God's Kingdom and for the Holy Father's monthly intention. This habit of prayer encourages a Eucharistic spirituality of solidarity with the Body of Christ and loving service to others. Nourishing this spiritual program is the love of the Sacred Heart of Jesus." (www.apostleshipofprayer.org)

Traditional Morning Offering

O Jesus, through the Immaculate Heart of Mary, I offer you all my prayers, works, joys, and suffering of this day in union with the Holy Sacrifice of the Mass throughout the world. I offer them for all the intentions of your Sacred Heart: the salvation of souls, reparation for sin, the reunion of all Christians; I offer them for the intentions of our bishops, and all Apostles of Prayer, and in particular for those recommended by our Holy Father this month.

Devotion to Our Lady

Since St. Ignatius had such a strong commitment to and love of Jesus, it should come as no surprise that he also had a deep and abiding devotion to Mary, the mother of Jesus. A favorite prayerful request of his to Mary was: "Place me with your Son."

After his conversion, Ignatius went as a pilgrim to the shrine of Our Lady at Montserrat in Spain. He spent the night in prayer at the altar of Our Lady in the church and symbolically left his sword and dagger at the altar. Ignatius and his first companions chose the feast of Mary's assumption as the day for their first vows at Paris, and later he wanted the Basilica of St. Mary Major in Rome to be the place of his first Mass as a priest. The little office of Our Lady always remained a special prayer for him.

Mary has a prominent place in the Spiritual Exercises *of St. Ignatius. In key meditations (the* Meditation on Sin *and the* Two Standards*), Ignatius urges retreatants to make a colloquy to Our Lady, asking her to obtain for them from her Son the important graces sought. Mary is also frequently mentioned in the various mysteries of Christ's life that are contemplated in* *the course of the* Spiritual Exercises. *It has often been noted that the first contemplation of the fourth week that Ignatius suggests is Christ's apparition to Our Lady.*

Devotion to Our Lady continues to be an important element in the spiritual lives of the sons of Ignatius as well as in their ministries. For example, the Sodality of Mary historically has played a significant role in the schools of the Society of Jesus, and presently the Christian Life Communities continue in this tradition. The feast of the Assumption (August 15) is still one of the traditional days on which Jesuits pronounce their vows, and Mary has been officially designated the Queen of the Society of Jesus.

Colloquy with Mary

A colloquy should be made with Our Lady. I beg her to obtain for me grace to be received under the standard of her Son and Lord.

—Sp. Ex., #147

Speaking to Mary

We should try to speak, in all simplicity and with all the tenderness of our heart, with the Woman of the new and eternal covenant; speak to her of her Son, Our Lord Jesus Christ; speak to her about herself, the one full of grace, who became all service and love; and speak to her about ourselves who so desire with her to follow Christ.

—Karl Rahner, SJ

The Annunciation to Our Lady

First Point. The angel, St. Gabriel, greets Our Lady and announces to her the conception of Christ our Lord; "The angel entered the place where Mary was, greeted her, and said: 'Hail, full of grace. You will conceive in your womb and give birth to a Son.'"

Second Point. The angel confirms what he said to our Lady by telling her about the conception of St. John the Baptist: "And behold, Elizabeth, your relative, has also conceived a son in her old age."

Third Point. Our Lady replied to the angel: "Behold the handmaid of the Lord. Be it done to me according to your word."

—Sp. Ex., #262

First Apparition to Mary

He appeared to the Virgin Mary. Although this is not stated in Scripture, still it is considered as understood by the statement that he appeared to many others. For Scripture supposes that we have understanding, as it is written: "Are even you without understanding?" (Matt. 15:16).

—Sp. Ex., #299

Mary's Obedience

Along his pilgrim way from Loyola to Rome, Ignatius prayed unceasingly to Mary, Our Lady, asking her to obtain for him the grace to be received under the banner of her Son. In her expression, "Behold the servant of the Lord, let it be done to me according to your word," Mary shows us how to live in total availability and to place our whole lives at the service of her Son. In her instruction to the servants at Cana, "Do whatever he tells you," Mary points out for us the basic orientation that should guide our lives. For this reason, the Society has always seen in Mary a model of obedience.

—General Congregation 35, Decree 4

My Mother

O holy Mary, my Queen, I recommend myself to thy blessed protection and special keeping, and to the bosom of thy mercy, today and every day and at the hour of my death—my soul and my body I recommend to thee. I entrust to thee my hope and consolation, my distress and my misery, my life and its termination. Through thy most holy intercession and through thy merits may all my actions be directed according to thy will and that of thy Son. Amen.

—St. Aloysius Gonzaga, SJ (1568–91)

A Threefold Love

Daughter, bride, Mother—Mary was all these in her love for God. How would it have been possible for anyone else to fulfill the first commandment of Christ more perfectly than did Mary? If God showered upon Mary the threefold love of a Father, a bridegroom, and a Son, Mary answered each manifestation of His affection with the perfect complement.

—Daniel A. Lord, SJ

Holy Virgin

Holy Virgin, truly mother of the eternal Word who has come into our flesh and our life, Lady who conceived in faith and in your blessed womb the salvation of us all, and so are the mother of all the redeemed, you who live ever in God's life, near to us still, because those united to God are nearest to us.

—Karl Rahner, SJ

The May Magnificat

May is Mary's month and I
Muse at that and wonder why
    Her feasts follow reason
    Dated due to season—

Candlemas, Lady Day;
But the Lady Month, May,
    Why fasten that upon her,
    With a feasting in her honour?

Is it only its being brighter
Than the most are must delight her?
        Is it opportunest
        And flowers finds soonest?

Ask of her, the mighty mother:
Her reply puts this other
        Question: What is Spring?
        Growth in every thing—

Flesh and fleece, fur and feather,
Grass and greenworld all together;
        Star-eyed strawberry-breasted
        Throstle above her nested

Cluster of bugle blue eggs thin
Forms and warms the life within;
        And bird and blossom swell
        In sod or sheath or shell.

All things rising, all things sizing
Mary sees, sympathizing
        With that world of good
        Nature's motherhood.

Their magnifying of each its kind
With delight calls to mind
        How she did in her stored
        Magnify the Lord.

Well but there was more than this:
Spring's universal bliss
        Much, had much to say
        To offering Mary May.

When drop-of-blood-and-foam-dapple
Bloom lights the orchard-apple
  And thicket and thorp are merry
  With silver-surfèd cherry.

And azuring-over greybell makes
Wood banks and brakes wash wet like lakes
  And magic cuckoocall
  Caps, clears, and clinches all—

This ecstasy all through mothering earth
Tells Mary her mirth till Christ's birth
  To remember and exultation
  In God who was her salvation.
      —Gerard Manley Hopkins, SJ

Novena of Grace

St. Francis Xavier, a fellow student of St. Ignatius at Paris and one of his first companions, left for the Far East shortly after the founding of the Society. He never returned to Europe and his missionary activity would only come to an end with his death eleven years later, just off the coast of mainland China. A priest and missionary of great zeal and love of God, he was to become the greatest missionary of the church since the time of St. Paul.

Over the years Francis Xavier has remained a very popular saint through the Novena of Grace. Usually preached in churches throughout the world March 4–12 (just before the anniversary of his canonization), the novena has been a wonderful source of grace and blessings for those who sought the saint's intercession.

Traditional Novena Prayer

O most admirable and loving St. Francis Xavier, in union with you, we adore the Divine Majesty. While joyfully giving thanks to God for the wonderful graces, which God conferred upon you in life, and for the greater glory with which God has gifted you in heaven, we come to you with heartfelt love, asking you to secure for us by your powerful intercession, the inestimable blessings of living and dying in the state of grace. We also ask you to obtain the favors we seek in this novena.

(Pause for personal petitions)

But if what we ask is not for the glory of God, or for the good of our souls, obtain for us what is most conducive to both. Amen.

Prayer on Feast Day (December 3)

God our Father, by the preaching of Francis Xavier you brought many nations to yourself. Give his zeal for the faith to all who believe in you, that your Church may rejoice in continued growth throughout the world. Grant this through our Lord Jesus Christ, your Son, who lives and reigns with you and the Holy Spirit, one God, for ever and ever. Amen.

St. Francis Xavier's Final Days

At noon on Thursday he regained his senses, but spoke only to call upon the Blessed Trinity, Father, Son and Holy Ghost, always one of his tenderest devotions. I heard him again repeat the words: *Jesus Son of David, have mercy on me*, and he exclaimed again and again: *O Virgin Mother of God, remember me!* He continued to have these and similar words on his lips until the night of Friday passed on towards the dawn of Saturday, when I could see that he was dying and put a lighted candle in his hand. Then, with the name of Jesus on his lips he rendered his soul to his Creator and Lord with great repose and quietude.

From the account of a Chinese Christian interpreter

Our Way of Proceeding

In the Constitutions of the Society of Jesus, *St. Ignatius often used the term "way of proceeding." It refers to "certain attitudes, values, and patterns of behavior that join together to become what has been called the Jesuit way of proceeding" (General Congregation 34, Decree 26). The concluding decree of this recent congregation (1995) is entitled* Characteristics of Our Way of Proceeding. *This decree "sought to summarize certain characteristics from this way of proceeding that are particularly significant for the new situations and changing ministries of contemporary times." The following character- istics are highlighted: deep personal love for Jesus Christ; contemplative in action; an apostolic body in the Church; in solidarity with those most in need; partnership with others; called to learned ministry; men sent, always available for new missions; and ever searching for the* Magis.

Our Way of Proceeding

Lord, meditating on "our way of proceeding," I have discovered that the ideal of *our* way of acting is *your* way of acting.

Give me that *sensus Christi* that I may feel with your feeling, with the sentiments of your heart, which basically are love for your Father and love for all men and women.

Teach me how to be compassionate to the suffering, to the poor, the blind, the lame, and the lepers.

Teach us your way so that it becomes our way today, so that we may come closer to the great ideal of St. Ignatius: to be companions of Jesus, collaborators in the work of redemption.

—Pedro Arrupe, SJ

Jesuit Identity

What is it to be a companion of Jesus today? It is to engage, under the standard of the Cross, in the crucial struggle of our time: the struggle for faith and that struggle for justice which it includes.

—General Congregation 32, Decree 2

For the Greater Glory of God

We should recall that mediocrity has no place in Ignatius' world view; he demands leaders in service to others in building the Kingdom of God in the market place of business and ideas, of service, of law and justice, of economics, theology and all areas of human life. He urges us to work for the greater glory of God because the world desperately needs men and women of competence and conscience who generously give of themselves for others.

—Peter-Hans Kolvenbach, SJ

Bond of Love

God is love, and so we too love. God is mercy, and so we too show mercy. God is good, and so we too desire to be good. If we do not love, we really do not have anything to say. Here we discover the root and source of our identity and our mission.

—Adolfo Nicolás, SJ

A Spirituality of Aging and Dying

Although the "way of proceeding" is mainly marked by humble, loving, and generous apostolic service for God's greater glory, it should be noted, in this age of longer life expectancy, that a Jesuit can and should continue his mission, mainly through prayer and sacrifice, during the less active and declining years of his life and at the time of death.

*The important role of a "spirituality of aging and dying"
should be kept in mind in this "way of proceeding."*

In the Hands of God

More than ever, I now find myself in the hands of God.
This is what I have wanted all my life, from my youth. And
this is still the one thing I want. But now there is a difference:
the initiative is entirely with God. It is indeed a profound
spiritual experience to know and feel myself so totally in his
hands.

—Pedro Arrupe, SJ

Last Written Words

The good life does not have to be an easy one, as our
blessed Lord and saints have taught us. Pope John Paul II in
his later years used to say, "The Pope must suffer." Suffering
and diminishment are not the greatest evils, but are normal
ingredients in life, especially in old age. They are to be
accepted as elements of a full human existence. Well into my
90th year I have been able to work productively. As I become
increasingly paralyzed and unable to speak, I can identify
with the many paralytics and mute persons in the Gospels,
grateful for the loving and skilled care I receive and for the
hope of everlasting life in Christ. If the Lord now calls me to
a period of weakness, I know his power can be made perfect
in infirmity. Blessed be the name of the Lord.

—Avery Dulles, SJ

It Is You Whom I Ever Sought

Lord, since with every instinct of my being and through
all the changing fortunes of my life, it is you whom I have
ever sought, you whom I have set at the heart of universal
matter, it will be in a resplendence which shines through all

things and in which all things are ablaze, that I shall have the felicity of closing my eyes.

—Pierre Teilhard de Chardin, SJ

Finding God

We must overcome death by finding God in it. And by the same token, we shall find the divine established in our innermost hearts, in the last stronghold which might have seemed able to escape his reach.

—Pierre Teilhard de Chardin, SJ

Looking Back at Age 85

I love this life because Christ has assured me that we who believe and love are tabernacles of the Trinity tented within us. I love the Eucharist for the Christ who, marvel of marvels, rests within me "body and blood, soul and divinity." I love my priesthood, the endless opportunities to play Christ the servant, particularly to his "little people," the poor and the powerless.

—Walter J. Burghardt, SJ

Suffering

Suffering, especially as we age, calls not only for faith but for a spirituality. All Christian spirituality is the response of a man or woman to God revealing divine love through Christ in the Spirit. In the concrete, it consists in knowing, loving, and serving God and God's children in the context of a community of faith, hope, and love. At its core, Christian spirituality is human love responding to divine love, to a God who "so loved the world that He gave His only Son" (Jn 3:16), not only to share our flesh but to experience our pain and die our death.

—Walter J. Burghardt, SJ

Letter to the Brethren

Here I am at the parting of the ways and I must take the other road after all. The death sentence has been passed and the atmosphere is so charged with enmity and hatred that no appeal has any hope of succeeding. The actual reason for my condemnation was that I happened to be, and chose to remain, a Jesuit....There was one underlying theme—a Jesuit is *a priori* an enemy of the Reich. So the whole proceedings turned into a sort of comedy developing a theme. It was not justice—it was simply the carrying out of the determination to destroy.

May God shield you all. I ask for your prayers. And I will do my best to catch up, on the other side, with all that I have left undone here on earth. Towards noon I will celebrate Mass once more and then in God's name take the road under his providence and guidance.

—Alfred Delp, SJ
(Alfred Delp was a German Jesuit imprisoned by the Nazis. After a mock trial, he was sentenced to death and hanged just before the end of World War II.)

Patience and Hope

I wait, O God, with patience and in hope. I wait like a blind man who has been promised the dawning of light. I await the resurrection of the dead and of the flesh.

—Karl Rahner, SJ

Closing

My brothers and sisters let us close on a quiet note, so that God's gentle yet powerful word of grace within us is not drowned by our loud and weak human words. Let us pray: "Lord, help my unbelief," give me the grace of faith in Jesus Christ our Lord, in his gospel and his saving power.

—Karl Rahner, SJ

Sources and Acknowledgments

Excerpts from the Spiritual Exercises are taken from *Ignatius of Loyola, Spiritual Exercises and Selected Works.* Edited by George E. Ganss, SJ. The Classics of Western Spirituality. New York/Mahwah, NJ: Paulist Press, 1991. Used with permission.

The poems of Gerard Manley Hopkins are taken from *The Poetical Works of Gerard Manley Hopkins.* Edited by Norman H. MacKenzie. New York: Oxford University Press, 1990.

With one exception, the prayers of Karl Rahner are taken from *Prayers for a Lifetime.* New York: Crossroad Publishing, 1984. Used with permission. The excerpt on p. 42 is from his *Spiritual Exercises.* New York: Herder and Herder, 1965.

Excerpts from General Congregations are taken from *Jesuit Life & Mission Today, The Decrees & Accompanying Documents of the 31st–35th General Congregations of the Society of Jesus.* John W. Padberg, SJ, editor. St. Louis: The Institute of Jesuit Sources, 2009.

The letter of St. Ignatius on p. 20 is from Ignatius of Loyola, *Letters and Instructions.* St. Louis: The Institute of Jesuit Sources, 2006. The two letters of Francis Xavier on pp. 21–22 are from *The Letters and Instructions of Francis Xavier.* Translated and introduced by M. Joseph Costelloe, SJ. St. Louis: The Institute of Jesuit Sources, 1992. The account of his death is from James Brodrick, SJ, *Saint*

Francis Xavier. New York: The Wickloo Press, 1952. The letter of Peter Faber on p. 22 is from Mary Purcell, *The Quiet Companion*. Chicago: Loyola University Press, 1970. The other two excerpts of Faber's are from his *Memoriale*. St. Louis: The Institute of Jesuit Sources, 1996.

The excerpts of Matteo Ricci are from his *On Friendship, One Hundred Maxims for a Chinese Prince*. Translated by Timothy Billings. New York: Columbia University Press, 2009. The excerpt of Joseph de Anchieta on p. 25 is from Joseph N. Tylenda, SJ, *Jesuit Saints and Martyrs*. Chicago: Loyola University Press, 1998. The excerpt of Edmund Campion on p. 25 is from Evelyn Waugh's *Edmund Campion*. San Francisco: Ignatius Press, 2005.

The excerpts of John de Brébeuf and Isaac Jogues are from *The Jesuit Relations and Allied Documents*. Edited by Reuben Gold Thwaites. Cleveland: The Burrows Brothers Co., 1898. The excerpts of Louis Lallemant are from his *Spiritual Teaching*. Edited by Alan G. McDougall. New York: Benziger Brothers, 1928. The excerpt "True Devotion" of Jean Nicolas Grou is from his *Manual for Interior Souls*. Westminister, MD: The Newman Press, 1955; the prayer "Come, O Divine Spirit" is from his *How to Pray*. London: Thomas Baker, 1898.

The two poems of Robert Southwell are from *The Complete Works of R. Southwell, SJ*. London: D. Stewart, Warwick Chambers, 1876. "Meditation: Eastern Point Retreat House" by Leonard J. McCarthy is from the archives of the College of the Holy Cross. "Jesus, Love of My Heart" by Francis W. Sweeney is from his *Morning Window, Evening Window*. London: Haggerton Press, 1999.

"I Love Your Promise/Psalm 119" by Daniel Berrigan is from his *Uncommon Prayer, A Book of Psalms*. Maryknoll, NY: Orbis Books, 1998. Used with permission of the author. The two poems of Thomas Flowers are from his *Walking Humbly: Scripture Meditations in Verse*. New York/Mahwah, NJ: Paulist Press, 2009. Used with permission.

Excerpts from Jean-Pierre de Caussade are from his *Abandonment to Divine Providence*. New York: Image Books (Doubleday), 1975.

The excerpts of Pierre Teilhard de Chardin "Priestly Prayer," "Saviour of Human Activity," "Immersed in God ," "It Is You Whom I Have Ever Sought," and "Finding God," are from *The Divine Milieu*. New York: Harper and Row, 1959. "Lord of the World" and "Patient Trust" are from his *Writings in Time of War*. New York: Harper and Row, 1960; the prayer "The Mass on the World" is from *Hymn of the Universe*. New York: Harper and Row, 1959.

The prayer of Fr. Pedro Arrupe on p. 73 is from his final address to the Society as General Superior (1983). His other excerpts are from *The Spiritual Legacy of Pedro Arrupe, SJ*. The New York Province, 1985 (Rome: Jesuit Curia, 1985). The quote of Fr. Peter-Hans Kolvenbach on p. 72 is from his address at the 5th Congress of Jesuit Alumni in Sydney, Australia, July, 1997. The quote of Fr. Adolfo Nicolás is from his homily at the closing Mass of General Congregation 35, March, 2008.

The excerpts on Devotion to the Sacred Heart (pp. 59–62) are from the booklet *A Most Pleasant Mission* published by the General Office of the Apostleship of Prayer in Rome, 1988.

The two prayers of Joseph Tetlow are from his *Choosing Christ in the World*. St. Louis: The Institute of Jesuit Sources, 1982. Used by permission: © The Institute of Jesuit Sources, St. Louis, MO. The prayer by John Veltri is from the site www.jesuits/ca/orientations.

The two excerpts of Avery Dulles on pp. 45–46 are from his autobiography, *A Testimonial to Grace & Reflection on a Theological Journey*. Kansas City, MO: Sheed and Ward, 1996. The excerpt "Last Written Words" is from his final McGinley lecture (see *America*, April 21, 2008, pp. 9–12).

The excerpt of Henri de Lubac is from his *The Splendor of the Church*. San Francisco: The Ignatius Press, 1986. The two excerpts of Bernard Lonergan are from his *A Second Collection*, edited by William F. J. Ryan and Bernard J. Tyrrell, Toronto: University of Toronto Press, 1974. The excerpts of Walter J. Burghardt are from his *Long Have I Loved You: A Theologian Reflects on His Church*. Maryknoll, NY: Orbis Books, 2000.

The two excerpts by Daniel A. Lord on p. 47 are from his *Letters to My Lord*. New York: Herder and Herder, 1969. The excerpt on p. 65 is from his *Our Lady in the Modern World*. St. Louis: The Queen's Work, 1940.

The letter of Alfred Delp is from *The Prison Meditations of Father Alfred Delp*. New York: Herder and Herder, 1963. The excerpt of Ignacio Ellacuría is cited from *The Ignatian Tradition: Spirituality in History* by Kevin F. Burke, SJ, and Eileen Burke Sullivan. Collegeville, MN: Liturgical Press, 2009.

The excerpt of Walter Ciszek, "God's Will," on p. 48 is from his *He Leadeth Me*. New York: Doubleday, 1973.

The excerpt of Richard J. Hauser is from his *In His Spirit: A Guide to Today's Spirituality*. New York/Mahwah, NJ: Paulist Press, 1982. The excerpts of James Martin are from his *Becoming Who You Are: Insights on the True Self from Thomas Merton & Other Saints*. New York/Mahwah, NJ: Paulist Press, 2006. The excerpts of William A. Barry are from his book *God and You, Prayer as a Personal Relationship*. New York/Mahwah, NJ: Paulist Press, 1987. All used with permission. The excerpt of George A. Aschenbrenner is from his *Stretched for Greater Glory: What to Expect From the Spiritual Exercises*. Chicago: Loyola University Press, 2004.

A number of traditional Jesuit prayers can be found in the *Liber Devotionum*, published by the Missouri Province of the Society of Jesus, 1947. (The prayer of Peter Canisius, "Prayer for the Society," and the prayer of Aloysius Gonzaga, "My Mother," are taken from here.) Also *For Jesuits*, edited by John Hardon, SJ. Chicago: Loyola

University Press, 1963. (The two prayers of Claude la Columbière on pp. 30–31 are taken from this source.) There is also the more recent *Hearts on Fire: Praying with Jesuits*. Edited by Michael Harter, SJ. St. Louis: Institute of Jesuit Sources, 1993.

The excerpt of William Hewett on pp. 53–54 is from his *Inigo: Full Text*. London: Inigo International Centre, 1985 (william.hewett@campion.ox.ac.uk). Copyright by the author; reprinted with permission.